Melanie Graham • Stanton Procter

Workbook

1

2nd Edition

T0347347

OXFORD
UNIVERSITY PRESS

Great Clarendon Street, Oxford OX2 6DP

Oxford University Press is a department of the University of Oxford.
It furthers the University's objective of excellence in research, scholarship,
and education by publishing worldwide in

Oxford New York

Auckland Cape Town Dar es Salaam Hong Kong Karachi
Kuala Lumpur Madrid Melbourne Mexico City Nairobi
New Delhi Shanghai Taipei Toronto

With offices in

Argentina Austria Brazil Chile Czech Republic France Greece
Guatemala Hungary Italy Japan Poland Portugal Singapore
South Korea Switzerland Thailand Turkey Ukraine Vietnam

OXFORD and OXFORD ENGLISH are registered trade marks of
Oxford University Press in the UK and in certain other countries

ISBN: 978 0 19 400504 3

Printed in China

This book is printed on paper from certified and well-managed sources.

ACKNOWLEDGEMENTS

Cover illustration by: Paul Gibbs

Illustrations by: Yvette Banek, Shirley Beckes/Craven Design, Terri and Joe
Chicko, Rachel Fuller, Anne Iosa, Stephanie Peterson, Mark Ruffle, Zina
Saunders, Susan Simon, Jim Talbot.

*The Publishers would like to thank the following for their kind permission to reproduce
photographs and other copyright material*: Alamy Stock Photo (Nigel Cattlin);
Getty Images (BruceBlock/E+, ElementalImaging/E+, Mac99/iStock);
Shutterstock (Cathy Keifer, DenisNata, Ekler, Ewais, Huyangshu, Maria
Kazakova1).

Original characters developed by: Amy Wummer

The Alphabet

Trace and write.

 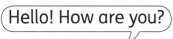 

A. Read and match.

1. Good morning.   2. Hello! How are you?   3. Fine, thank you.

B. Look and write.

Hello   are   morning   thank

1. Good _____.

2. ___! How ___ you?

3. Fine, ___ you.

Annie   Ted   Digger   girl   boy   dog

A. Look and match.

1.
2.
3.
4.
5.
6.

Annie   Ted   Digger

girl   boy   dog

B. Write the letter.

1. ____b____ Annie

2. _____ Ted

3. _____ Digger

4. _____ boy

5. _____ girl

6. _____ dog

I'm Annie. I'm a girl.

You're Ted. You're a boy.

A. Look and match.

1.    2.    3.    4.    5.    6.

I'm Digger. I'm a dog.

You're Annie. You're a girl.

You're Ted. You're a boy.

I'm Ted. I'm a boy.

You're Digger. You're a dog.

I'm Annie. I'm a girl.

B. Your turn. Draw and write.

I'm _____ .

I'm a _____ .

Phonics Time

| ball | pencil | boy | pizza | bird | pen |

A. Does it begin with b or p? Look and circle.

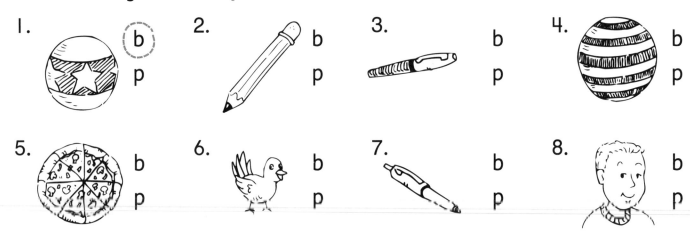

1. b / p
2. b / p
3. b / p
4. b / p
5. b / p
6. b / p
7. b / p
8. b / p

B. Match and say.

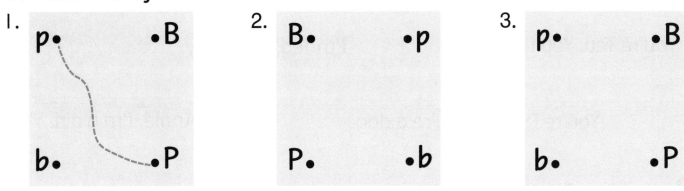

1.
p•   •B

b•   •P

2.
B•   •p

P•   •b

3.
p•   •B

b•   •P

C. Look and write.

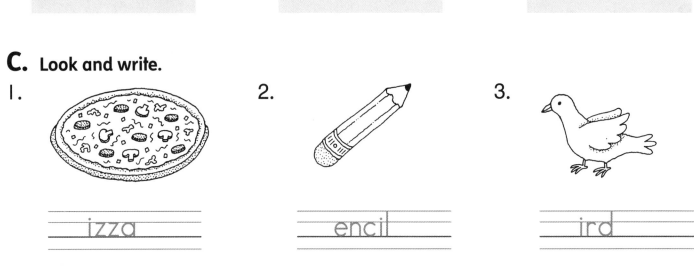

1. ____izza____

2. ____encil____

3. ____ird____

A. Read and match.

1. Ah-choo!

2. Bless you!

3. Thanks.

B. Unscramble, match, and write.

1. lsseb ouy •   • Ah-choo!

2. kahtns •   • Bless you!   Bless you!

3. ha-ocoh •   • Thanks.

| butterfly | tree | bird | lake | flower | cloud |

A. Look and circle.

1.  (lake) cloud

2.  tree flower

3.  bird butterfly

4.  flower cloud

5.  flower lake

6.  bird tree

B. Look and write.

1. 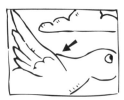 _____

2.  _____

3.  _____

4.  _____

5.  _____

6.  _____

This is a butterfly.

That's a bird.

A. Look and circle.

1.  this / that

2.  this / that

3.  this / that

4.  this / that

B. Look and write.

1. _____ is a _____.

2. _____

3. _____

4. _____

C. Your turn. Draw and write.

This _____

That's _____

 kite  girl  kangaroo   key  gorilla   garden

A. Does it begin with g or k? Circle and write.

1.  g (k)

key

2.  g k

_____

3. 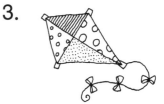 g k

_____

B. Which pictures begin with the same sound? Circle.

1.

2.

3.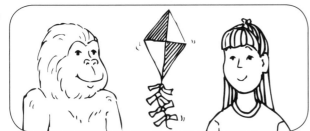

4.

C. Match and say.

1.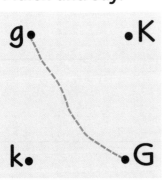
g•   •K
k•   •G

2.
k•   •G
g•   •K

3.
G•   •g
K•   •k

A. Read and match.

1. Sh! Be quiet!

2. Sorry.

3. That's okay.

B. Look and write.

okay   quiet   Sorry   .

1. Sh! Be _____ !

2. _____

3. That's _____ .

Word Time

 sheep  horse  cow   chicken   goat   cat

A. Look and match.

1.  2. 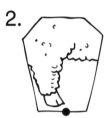 3.  4.  5. 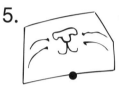 6.

sheep horse goat cat chicken cow

B. Find and circle.

horhorseckpicattgmslagoatchsheepfambccowchickenrhose

C. Unscramble and write.

1. h p s e e   _sheep_

2. t a c   _____

3. o t a g   _____

4. e h r o s   _____

5. h e c k c i n   _____

6. o w c   _____

A. Look and write.

1.

   What's _____ ?   It's _____ .

2.

3.

4.

5.

6.

B. Your turn. Draw and write.

What's _____ ?

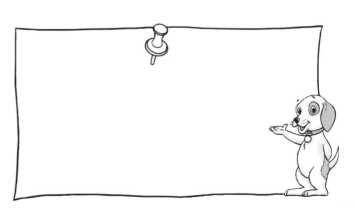

Phonics Time

 nurse  mother 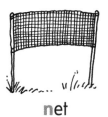 net  milk  mop  night

A. Which picture begins with the letter? Write ✓.

1. **m** 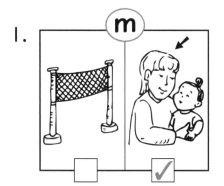 ☐ ✓

2. **n**  ☐ ☐

3. **m**  ☐ ☐

4. **n** 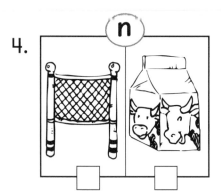 ☐ ☐

5. **n**  ☐ ☐

6. **m**  ☐ ☐

B. Which pictures begin with the letter? Circle.

m

n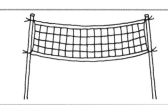

A. Look and match.

1.
2.
3.
4.
5.
6.

You're a dog.   That's a horse.   This is a butterfly.

I'm Ted.   What's that?
It's a bird.   I'm a girl.

B. Look and circle.

1.

won   sow   cow

2.

cat   tac   cab

3.

bred   bird   drab

4.

kale   leak   lake

5.

girl   hurl   grill

6.

tee   tree   three

A. Look at the numbers. Write the sentence.

1 a	2 I'm	3 is	4 you	5 You're
6 Annie	7 morning	8 This	9 are	10 Thanks.
11 Good	12 tree	13 girl	14 boy	15 How
16 That's	17 flower	18 ?	19 .	20 Ted

1. 11 7 19 15 9 4 18

Good _____

2. 2 6 19 2 1 13 19

_____

3. 5 20 19 5 1 14 19

_____

4. 8 3 1 17 19 16 1 12 19

_____

B. Which picture begins with a different sound? Write ✗.

1.

2.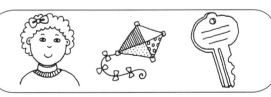

3.

4.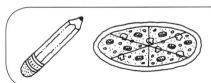

| bee | caterpillar | fly | spider |

A. Read and match.

1. bee •

2. caterpillar •

3. fly •

4. spider •

B. Look and write.

1. caterpillar

2. _____

3. _____

4. _____

Here you are. Thanks. You're welcome.

A. Look and write.

Thanks   welcome   you   .

1.

Here _____ are.

2.

_____

3.

You're _____ .

B. Unscramble, match, and write.

1. oyu're celwemo •   • Here you are.   _____

2. eehr oyu rea •   • Thanks.   _____

3. haktns •   • You're welcome.   _____

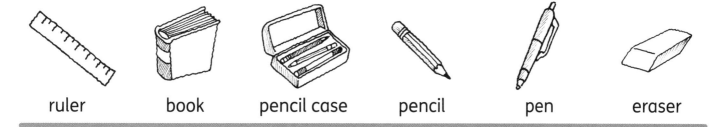

ruler | book | pencil case | pencil | pen | eraser

A. Write the letter.

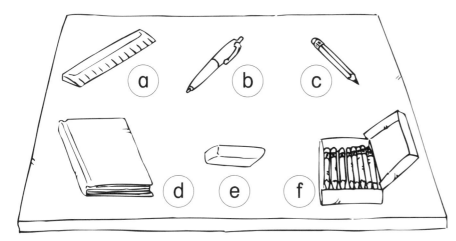

1. ___d___ book

2. _____ eraser

3. _____ pen

4. _____ pencil

5. _____ pencil case

6. _____ ruler

B. Read the question. Write the answer.

1. What's this?

It's a

2. What's this?

3. What's this?

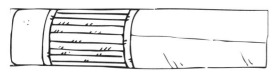

4. What's this?

Practice Time

A. Look and circle.

1.  a (pencil) an

2. 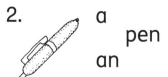 a pen an

3. 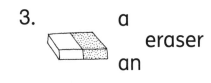 a eraser an

4. 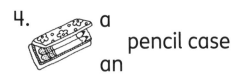 a pencil case an

5. 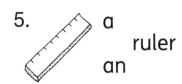 a ruler an

6. 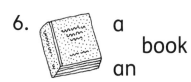 a book an

B. Read the question. Write the answer.

1. Is it a book?

_____

2. Is it a ruler?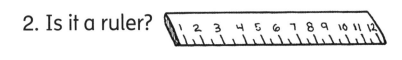

_____

3. Is it an eraser?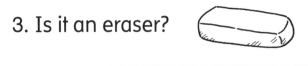

_____

4. Is it a pencil?

_____

dog   tiger   desk   teacher   duck   table

A. Does it begin with d or t? Write the word.

d words   desk

t words

B. What letter does it begin with? Read and write ✓.

d										
t	✓									
b										
p										
g										
k										
m										
n										

 What's your first name? Annie. What's your last name?  Day.

A. Look and write.

last   Lee   name   ?   Ted   What's   .   your

1.     *What's your first name?*

2.

B. Look and circle.

Tommy Lin

1. What's your first / last name?    Tommy.

2. What's your first / last name?    Lin.

C. Your turn. Read the question. Write the answer.

What's your first name?

What's your last name?

1	one	2	two	3	three
4	four	5	five	6	six
7	seven	8	eight	9	nine
10	ten	11	eleven	12	twelve

A. Write the number.

1. one ___1___   2. four _____   3. eleven _____   4. six _____

B. Write the word.

1. 12 ___twelve___   2. 8 _____   3. 2 _____

4. 7 _____   5. 3 _____   6. 10 _____

C. Look and match.

1.   2.   3. 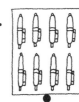 4.  5. 6.

two trees   one boy   five cows

eight pens   four dogs   twelve birds

D. Find and circle the numbers.

twetwelvethonevevininehtelevenonfourixsevenen

How many pencils?

Four pencils.

A. Count and write.

1. six goats

2.

3.

4.

B. Look and write.

1. How many books?

2.

3.

4.

Phonics Time

water   hand   woman   house   window   horse

A. Does it begin with h or w? Look and match.

1. 2. 3. 4. 5. 6.

w   h

B. Match and say.

1. h• •H
   w• •W

2. W• •h
   H• •w

3. h• •W
   w• •H

C. Does it begin with h or w? Circle and write.

1. h w _____
2.  h w _____
3. h w _____
4. h w _____
5. h w _____
6. h w _____

Ouch!

Are you okay? I think so.

A. Read and match.

1. Ouch!

2. Are you okay?

3. I think so.

B. Unscramble and match.

1. ear oyu kaoy •

2. i hkint os •

3. chou •

• Ouch!

• Are you okay?

• I think so.

C. Circle and write.

1. !ouch
   Ouch!
   ouch!

2. are you okay?
   ?are you okay
   Are you okay?

3. !I think so
   I think so.
   i think so.

happy

sad

hot

cold

hungry

thirsty

A. Look and write.

1.

2.

3.

4.

5.

6.

B. Read and complete the pictures.

I'm cold.

I'm happy.

I'm sad.

I'm hot.

C. Your turn. Draw and write.

I'm

Practice Time

A. Look and write.

1. _____ hungry?

2. _____ cold?

3. _____ happy?

4. _____ thirsty?

B. Your turn. Read the question. Write the answer.

1. Are you happy? _____

2. Are you sad? _____

Phonics Time

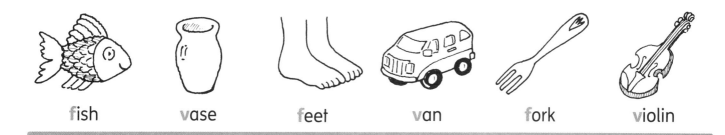

| fish | vase | feet | van | fork | violin |

A. Which pictures begin with the letter? Circle.

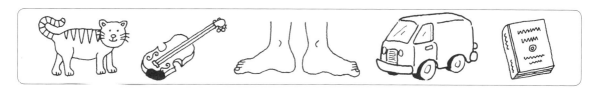

B. Look and write.

1.

2.

3.

4.

5.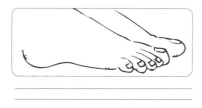

6.

C. Match and say.

d n k p b w f t g m v h

G M T F P N D K V W H B

A. Look and match.

1.

2.

3.

4.

5.

- Sh! Be quiet!

- Good morning.

- Here you are!

- What's your first name?
  Annie.

- Ouch!

B. Write the letter.

1. _____ book

2. _____ happy

3. _____ flower

4. _____ hot

5. _____ pencil

6. _____ ruler

A. Read and circle the mistakes.

1.

good morning?

my name is Ted.

what's your first name.

2.

this is a butterfly.

what's that!

is it a cloud.

3.

hello.

how are you.

are you hungry.

4.

this is an eraser?

is it a pen.

no! it isn't. it's a pencil!

B. Complete the puzzle.

ACROSS →

1.

2.

3.

4.

5.

DOWN ↓

1.

2.

3.

4.

5.

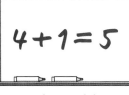

math problem

plus   equals   minus

A. Read and circle.

1. Three | minus / plus | four equals seven.

2. One plus one equals two is a | minus / math | problem.

3. Ten minus two | equals / plus | eight.

4. Eleven | plus / minus | five equals six.

B. Look and write.

1. **12 − 7 = 5**   Twelve minus seven equals five.

2. **4 + 6 = 10**

3. **6 − 4 = 2**

4. **8 + 3 = 11**

A. Circle and write.

1. Are _____ finished?

    you   Ted   I

2. No, _____ yet.

    net   not   night

3. Please _____ !

    happy   house   hurry

B. Read and connect.

1. Are   hurry   finished   ?

2. No,   you   yet   .

3. Please   not   !

pizza   burgers   salad   spaghetti   fish   rice

A. Look and match.

1.
2.
3.
4.
5.
6.

spaghetti   rice   salad   fish   burgers   pizza

    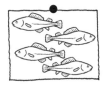 

B. Unscramble and write.

1. dsala

2. ifhs

3. igstetahp

4. zazip

5. eusgrrb

6. crie

C. Find and circle.

 pizzalingsspaghettisushfishersilmburgersapricemilsalad

A. Read and write ✓ or ✗.

- [ ] 1. I don't like spaghetti.
- [ ] 2. I like salad.
- [ ] 3. I like burgers.
- [ ] 4. I like pizza.
- [ ] 5. I don't like rice.
- [ ] 6. I don't like fish.

B. Unscramble and write.

1. don't / . / you / spaghetti / like

You _____ .

2. pizza / like / . / you

_____

C. Your turn. Draw and write.

Phonics Time

soup   zebra   sea   zipper   sock   zoo

A. Does it begin with s or z? Circle and write.

1.    s   z

2.   s   z

3.    s   z

B. Which picture begins with a different sound? Write X.

1.

2.

3.

4.

C. Which pictures begin with the letter? Circle.

S 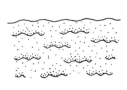

Z 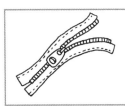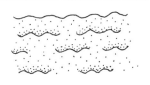

8

May I borrow a pen?

Sure. Here you are. Thanks.

A. Look and write.

are   borrow   Here   you   I   pencil   a   Thanks   .

1. May _____ ?

2. Sure. _____

3. _____

B. Circle and write.

1.

May I borrow a _____ ?

key   pen   ten

2.

_____ . Here you are.

Soup   Sea   Sure

3.

_____

Thanks   Three   Thirsty

Word Time

bananas

oranges

potatoes

apples

cucumbers

carrots

A. Count and write.

1. three apples

2.

3.

4.

5.

6.

B. Unscramble and write.

1. p e a l p s

2. o o t p a s e t

3. a b n a s a n

4. r t a c r s o

5. e g a r n o s

6. r s u u m c e c b

Do you like apples?

Yes, I do.

Do you like potatoes?

No, I don't.

A. Look and write.

1.  _____ carrots?

2.

3.

4.

B. Your turn. Read the question. Write the answer.

1. Do you like carrots?

2. Do you like apples?

 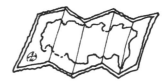

bag   ant   map   hat

A. Circle and write.

1.

bag
tag

_____
_____

2.

map
nap

_____
_____

3.

hat
bat

_____
_____

4.

ant
add

_____
_____

B. Circle the short a words.

1.
cow
sock
cat

2.
sad
hot
cold

3.
dog
bat
bird

4.
mop
pen
pan

5.
top
map
bed

C. Does it have short a? Circle.

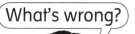   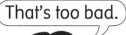 

What's wrong?   I feel sick.   That's too bad.

A. Circle and write.

1. What's _____?

      water   wrong   window

2. I feel _____.

      sock   soup   sick

3. That's too _____.

      bag   bad   bat

B. Unscramble, match, and write.

1. i efle kics •　　• What's wrong?   _____

2. s'hatt oto bda •　　• I feel sick.   _____

3. t'sawh grown •　　• That's too bad.   _____

| tall | short | fat | thin | young | old |

A. Circle and write.

1. young old
_____

2. short tall
_____

3. short fat
_____

4. thin fat
_____

5. tall short
_____

6. old young
_____

B. Write the letter.

1. _____ a fat cat

2. _____ an old goat

3. _____ a short girl

4. _____ a tall boy

5. _____ a young dog

6. _____ a thin cow

She's young. She isn't old.

He's thin. He isn't fat.

A. Look and match.

1.
2.
3.
4.
5.
6.

He's fat. He isn't thin.

She's old. She isn't young.

She's short. She isn't tall.

He's young. He isn't old.

She's thin. She isn't fat.

He's tall. He isn't short.

B. Look and write.

1.

2.

3.

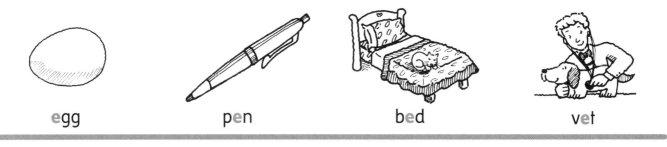

egg   pen   bed   vet

A. Look and write.

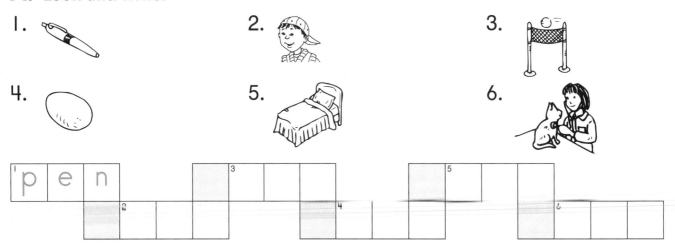

1.   2.   3.

4.   5.   6.

| 1 | | | | | 3 | | | | | 5 | | | | | |
| p | e | n | | | | | | | | | | | | | |

B. Which pictures have the vowel sound? Circle.

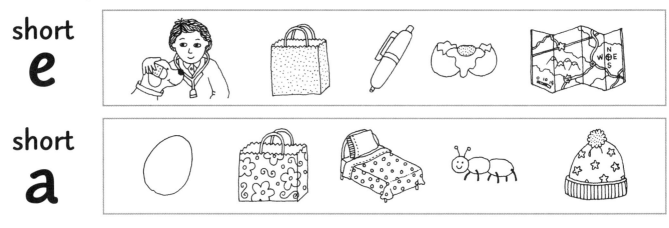

short **e**

short **a**

C. Circle the words you can read.

How many words can you read? _____

egg pen pan hat mad beg net Sam pen get fed bat men pet dad van hem

Review 3

A. Read and connect.

1. May I borrow a pen? •   • No, not yet. •   • That's too bad.

2. What's wrong? •   • Sure. Here you are. •   • Thanks.

3. Are you finished? •   • I feel sick. •   • Please hurry!

4. Ouch! •   • Thanks. •   • I think so.

5. Here you are. •   • Are you okay? •   • You're welcome.

B. Look and write.

1. _____   2. _____   3. _____

4. _____   5. _____   6. _____

7. _____   8. _____   9. _____

10. _____   11. _____   12. _____

A. Read and circle the mistakes.

1.
what's that.
it's pizza?
i don't like pizza?

2.
i like apples!
do you like apples.
yes, i do?

3.
i'm annie.
i'm a girl?
i'm young?

4.
this is ted?
he's young.
he isn't old?

B. Read and match.

1. three tall trees   2. two short boys   3. two old dogs   4. one fat man

C. Look and match.

1.    2.    3.    4.

I like apples.   He's tall. He isn't short.

You don't like oranges.   He's hungry. He isn't thirsty.

 rice paddy    plant    orange grove    potato field    cow pasture    animal

A. Read and match.

1. cow •   • field •

2. orange •   • paddy •

3. potato •   • pasture •

4. rice •   • grove •

B. Read. Circle the incorrect word. Write.

1.  Look! It's an orange (field).   *grove*

2.  This is a rice pasture.

3.  And that's a cow grove.

4.  It's a potato paddy.

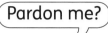

A. Read the question. Write the answer.

612-4321

761-3942

881-9841

235-6011

What's your telephone number?

1. _____

2. _____

3. _____

4. _____

B. Read and circle.

1. What's | you / yellow / your | telephone | name? / number? / nurse?

2. It's 769-1485.

3. Pencil / Please / Pardon | me?

4. 769-1485.

C. Your turn. Read the question. Write the answer.

What's your telephone number? _____

| police officer | nurse | mail carrier | teacher | firefighter | doctor |

A. Which picture is different? Circle and write.

1.
_____
_____

2.
_____
_____

3.
_____
_____

4.
_____
_____

5.
_____
_____

B. Look and write.

1.
He's a _____ .

2.
_____

3.
_____

4.
_____

Practice Time

Is he a doctor? Yes, he is.

Is she a teacher?

No, she isn't. She's a firefighter.

A. Read the question. Write the answer.

1. Is he a teacher?

_____

_____

2. Is she a firefighter?

_____

_____

3. Is he a mail carrier?

_____

_____

4. Is she a doctor?

_____

_____

B. Look and write.

1.

_____ nurse?

No, _____.

2.

_____ police officer?

_____

dig

sit

pin

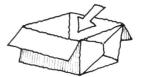
in

A. Look and write.

i	s	p	n	d	g	c	k	t

1.

tick

2.

3.

4.

5.

6.

7.

8.

B. Circle the short i words.

1.
pen
pin
pan

2.
in
on
an

3.
Sam
set
sip

4.
dig
peg
pat

5.
is
sad
sit

C. Does it have short i? Write ✓ or ✗.

1. ☐

2. ☐

3.  ☐

4.  ☐

5.  ☐

6.   ☐

Dad, this is my friend, Tom.

Nice to meet you, Tom. Hello.

A. Look and write.

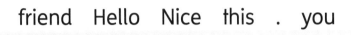
friend   Hello   Nice   this   .   you

1. Dad, _____ is my _____, Sam.

2. _____ to meet _____, Sam.

3. _____

B. Unscramble and write.

1. my / , / Pam / Mom / . / is / , / this / friend

   Mom, this is _____

2. Pam / . / you / meet / , / to / Nice

3. . / Hello

draw a picture

 play basketball

 drive a car

 ride a bike

 climb a tree

 sing a song

A. Look and circle.

1.

drive
ride   a bike

2.

sing
play   a song

3.

climb
play   basketball

4.

drive
sing   a car

5.

play
climb   a tree

6.

drive
draw   a picture

B. Complete the puzzle.

1.
2.
3.
4.
5.
6.

1. r i d e   a   b i k e

What is the mystery word? _____

Practice Time

I can ride a bike.

You can't ride a bike.

He can play basketball.

She can't play basketball.

A. Look and circle.

1. | She
He | can
can't | draw a picture.
ride a bike.
sing a song. |

2. | I
You
It | can
can't | drive a car.
ride a bike.
climb a tree. |

3. | I
You
It | can
can't | draw a picture.
climb a tree.
play basketball. |

B. Look and write.

1.    You _____ .

2.    He _____ .

3.   It _____ .

   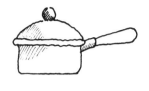

on　　　　　mop　　　　　hot　　　　　pot

A. Look and write.

1. 　2. 　3. 　4. 　5. 　6.

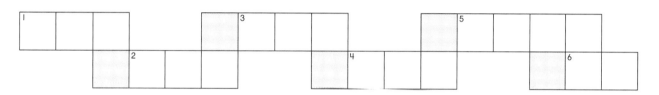

B. Circle the short o words.

1.
hit
hot
hat

2.
Sam
dot
bed

3.
fig
map
Tom

4.
pot
pat
pit

5.
dad
mop
pin

C. Which pictures have the vowel sound? Circle.

short **a**

short **e**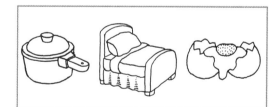

short **i**

short **o**

Conversation Time

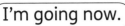

I'm going now. | Bye-bye! | See you tomorrow.

A. Read and match.

1. I'm going now.

2. Bye-bye!

3. See you tomorrow.

B. Circle and write.

1. i'm going now.

   I'm going now.

   I'm going now?

2. Bye-bye!

   bye-bye?

   !bye-bye

3. see you tomorrow.

   ?See you tomorrow

   See you tomorrow.

Word Time

 fly a kite  use a fork   make a sandwich  swim  play the guitar  do a cartwheel

A. Circle and write.

1.

make
fly   a sandwich

_____

2.

do
play   the guitar

_____

3.

use
do   a cartwheel

_____

4.

play
fly   a kite

_____

B. Unscramble and write.

1. od a rlecwetha

_____

2. kema a chasdiwn

_____

3. eus a kofr

_____

4. lyf a tiek

_____

5. miws

_____

6. lyap het ritagu

_____

A. Read the question. Check (✓) the correct answer.

1. Can she do a cartwheel?

☐ Yes, she can.

☐ No, she can't.

2. Can he play the guitar?

☐ Yes, he can.

☐ No, he can't.

3. Can it swim?

☐ Yes, it can.

☐ No, it can't.

4. Can he use a fork?

☐ Yes, he can.

☐ No, he can't.

B. Look and write.

1.

Can she _____ ?

Yes, _____ .

2.

3.

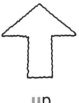
up

bus

nut

sun

A. Find and circle.

s	a	n	e	t
u	b	u	s	a
v	e	s	u	n
z	n	u	p	o
n	u	t	a	t

B. Circle the short u words and pictures.

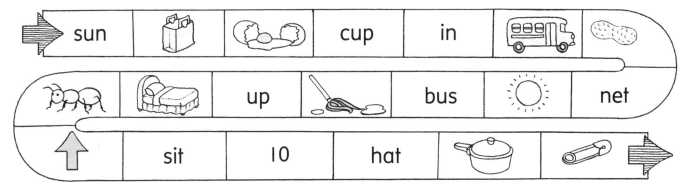

sun | cup | in

up | bus | net

sit | 10 | hat

C. Does it have short u? Circle and write.

1.  _____

2. 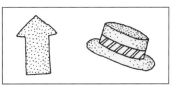 _____

3. 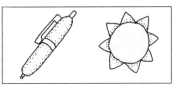 _____

4. 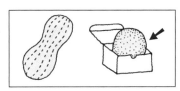 _____

A. Circle the mistakes. Then rewrite the sentences.

1. ⓢee ⓨou tomorrow⟨?⟩

   See you tomorrow.

2. dad. this is My friend! kim.

3. what's your Telephone number.

B. Look and write.

1.

   _can_____.

2.

   _She's_____.

3.

   _can_____.

4.

C. Read and match.

1. Can she drive a car?
   No, she can't.

3. Is she a doctor?
   Yes, she is.

2. You can't swim.

4. I can swim.

A. Look and write.

1.

2.

3.

4.

5.

6.

7.

8.

B. Read the question. Write the answer.

1. Can she fly a kite?

2. Is she a mail carrier?

3. Can she swim?

C. Your turn. Draw and write what you can do.

I can

 soil  seed  root  trunk  branch 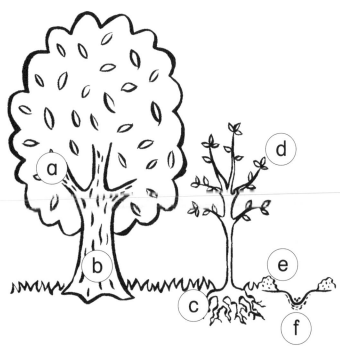 leaf

A. Look and write.

1. _e_____ soil

2. _____ root

3. _____ leaf

4. _____ seed

5. _____ branch

6. _____ trunk

B. Read the question. Write the answer.

1.  What is this?

_____
_____

2. 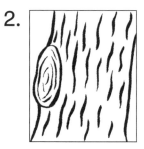 Is it a trunk?

_____
_____

3.  Is it a root?

_____
_____

4.  What is it?

_____
_____

A. Read and connect.

1. Ah-choo! •   • Thanks. •   • That's okay.

2. Good morning. •   • No, not yet. •   • Thank you.

3. Here you are. •   • Hello! How are you? •   • You're welcome.

4. Sh! Be quiet! •   • Bless you! •   • Fine, thank you.

5. Are you finished? •   • Sorry. •   • Please hurry!

B. Read and connect.

1. What's wrong? •   • Nice to meet you, Sue. •   • I think so.

2. Ouch! •   • Thanks.

                        • Bye-bye. •

3. May I borrow a pen? •   • That's too bad.

                        • Are you okay? •

                                                • Hello.

4. I'm going now. •   • I feel sick. •

                                                • See you tomorrow.

5. Dad, this is my friend, Sue. •   • Sure. Here you are. •

A. Complete the puzzle.

ACROSS   1.   2.   3.   4. **4**   5.   6.

DOWN

1.

2.

3.

4.

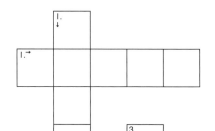
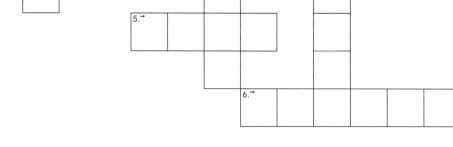

B. Which picture is different? Write X.

1.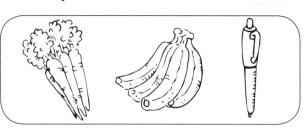

2.

3.

4.

A. Read and match.

1. What's that? •   • Twelve books.

2. I'm Annie. I'm a girl. •   • She can ride a bike.

3. Is it a pen? •   • It's a horse.

4. He can swim. •   • Yes, I am.

5. How many books? •   • You're Ted. You're a boy.

6. Are you happy? •   • No, it isn't. It's a pencil.

B. Read and match.

1. Do you like bananas? •   • She isn't tall.

2. This is a lake. •   • You don't like burgers.

3. Is he a teacher? •   • Yes, he can.

4. I like pizza. •   • No, I don't.

5. Can he swim? •   • No, he isn't. He's a doctor.

6. She's short. •   • That's a tree.

Phonics Time Review

A. Circle the words you can read.

How many words can you read? _____

cat hat ant pen bed vet in sit dig hot pot on mop sun nut bus up

B. Which picture begins with a different sound? Write X.

1.

2.
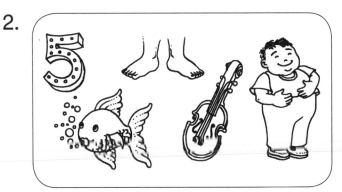

3.

4.

C. Match and say.

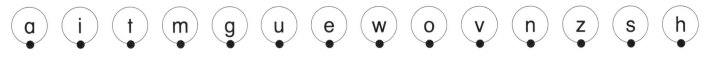

a i t m g u e w o v n z s h

T G V O Z A H M S W U N I E

Word List

A

a	page 3
ah-choo	5
am	26
an	18
animal	45
Annie	2
ant	38
apples	36
are	1

B

bad	39
bag	38
ball	4
bananas	36
basketball	51
be quiet	9
bed	42
bee	15
bike	52
bird	4
bless you	5
book	17
borrow	35
boy	2
branch	60
burgers	32
bus	59
butterfly	6
bye-bye	54

C

can	52
can't	52
car	51
carrots	36
cartwheel	55
cat	10
caterpillar	15

chicken	10
cloud	6
climb a tree	51
cold	25
cow	10
cow pasture	45
cucumbers	36

D

dad	50
desk	19
dig	49
Digger	2
do	37
do a cartwheel	55
doctor	47
dog	2
don't	33
draw a picture	51
drive a car	51
duck	19

E

egg	42
eight	21
eleven	21
equals	30
eraser	17

F

fat	40
feel	39
feet	27
fine	1
finished	31
firefighter	47
first	20
fish	27
five	21
flower	6

fly	15
fly a kite	55
fork	27
four	21
friend	50

G

garden	8
girl	2
goat	10
going	54
good morning	1
gorilla	8
guitar	55

H

hand	23
happy	26
hat	38
he	41
hello	1
here you are	16
he's	41
hot	25
horse	10
house	23
how are you	1
hungry	25
hurry	31

I

I think so	24
I'm	3
in	49
is	7
isn't	18
it	18
it's	11

K

kangaroo	8
key	8
kite	8

L

lake	6
last	20
leaf	60
like	33

M

mail carrier	47
make a sandwich	55
many	22
map	38
math problem	30
may	35
me	46
meet	50
milk	12
minus	30
mop	12
morning	1
mother	12
my	50

N

name	20
net	12
nice to meet you	50
night	12
nine	21
no	18
not	26
not yet	31
now	54
number	46
nurse	12
nut	57

O

okay	9
old	40
on	53
one	21
orange grove	45
oranges	36
ouch	24

P

pardon me	46
pen	4
pencil	4
pencil case	17
picture	51
pin	49
pizza	4
plant	45
play basketball	51
play the guitar	55
please	31
plus	30
police officer	47
pot	53
potato field	45
potatoes	36

R

rice	32
rice paddy	45
ride a bike	51
root	60
ruler	17

S

sad	25
salad	32
Sam	50
sandwich	55
sea	34
seed	60
see you tomorrow	54
seven	21
she	41
sheep	10
she's	41
short	40
sick	39
sing a song	51
sit	49
six	21
so	24
sock	34
soil	60
song	51
sorry	9
soup	34
spaghetti	32
spider	15
sun	57
sure	35
swim	55

T

table	19
tall	40
teacher	19
Ted	2
telephone	46
ten	21
thanks	5
thank you	1
that	11
that's	7
that's too bad	39
thin	40
think	24
thirsty	25
this	7
three	21
tiger	19
to	50
tomorrow	54
too	39
tree	6
trunk	60
twelve	21
two	21

U

up	57
use a fork	55

V

van	27
vase	27
vet	42
violin	27

W

water	23
welcome	16
what's	11
what's wrong	39
window	23
woman	23
wrong	39

Y

yes	18
yet	31
you	1
young	40
you're	3
you're welcome	16

Z

zebra	34
zipper	34
zoo	34